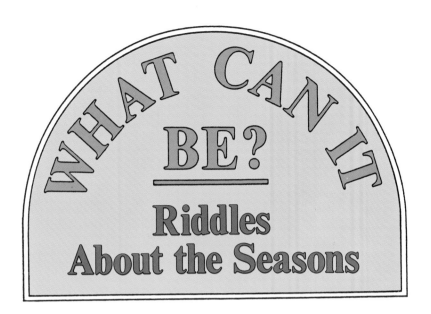

WHAT CAN IT BE?
Riddles About the Seasons

Jacqueline A. Ball

Silver Press

Published by Silver Press, a division of
Silver Burdett Press, Inc.
Simon & Schuster, Inc.
Prentice Hall Bldg., Englewood Cliffs, NJ 07632.

Printed in the United States of America.
10   9   8   7   6   5   4   3   2   1

Library of Congress Cataloging-in-Publication Data

Ball, Jacqueline A.,   Date.
Riddles about the Seasons
p.   cm.   (What can it be?)
Summary: A collection of rhyming riddles about
the characteristics of the four seasons.
1. Riddles, Juvenile.   2. Seasons——Juvenile humor.
[1. Riddles.   2. Seasons——Wit and humor.]
I. Title.   II. Series: Ball, Jacqueline A., What can it be?
PN6371.5.B27   1989   818′.5402——dc19

ISBN 0-671-68583-X   89-6067
ISBN 0-671-68582-1 (lib. bdg.)   CIP
                                          AC

WHAT CAN IT BE? concept created by Jacqueline A. Ball

PHOTO CREDITS:
Cover (clockwise from upper left): Hal Harrison/Grant Heilman Photography; Runk-Schoenberger/Grant Heilman Photography; Bruce Coleman, Inc./John Shaw; Barry L. Runk/Grant Heilman Photography.
Interior (in order of appearance): George H. Harrison/Grant Heilman Photography; LeFever-Grushow/Grant Heilman Photography; Bruce Coleman, Inc./Pat Lanza Field; Bruce Coleman, Inc./R. Llewellyn; Bruce Coleman, Inc./Barry Parker; Bruce Coleman, Inc./J. Markham; Bruce Coleman, Inc./Dr. Ivan Polunin; Grant Heilman/Grant Heilman Photography; EARTH SCENES/Zig Leszczynski; Larry LeFever/Grant Heilman Photography; Bruce Coleman, Inc./Joseph Van Wormer; Bruce Coleman, Inc./Carl Ziess; EARTH SCENES/Ralph A. Reinhold; Grant Heilman/Grant Heilman Photography; Bruce Coleman, Inc./Wayne Lankinen.
BOOK DESIGN
Cover: Helen Tullen, Nancy S. Norton
Interior: Nancy S. Norton

I'm in a blue egg,
Until
    Crick,
      Creak,
        CRACK!

Watch out earthworms,
It's time for a snack!

I'll eat
Then I'll sing.
I'm the first
Sign of spring.

What am I?

A ROBIN

Robins build
nests of twigs
and grasses
held together
by mud. The
mother robin
smears the mud
around the
inside of the
nest, using her
breast.

I have a bulb,
But I never light.
I come in colors
Bold and bright.
I sound like something
That kisses or sips.
You can't pick just one!
There are always ____.

TULIPS
(two lips)

Tulips and other spring flowers grow from bulbs planted underground. Bulbs store food and water so the buds inside can grow above ground and bloom.

Hear me whisper.
Hear me roar.
Hear me pound
The waves on shore.

Watch me billow.
Watch me whirl.
Watch me make
The weather vane twirl.

I can be frightening,
Or I can be fair.
But all that I am
Is a lot of air.

What am I?

THE WIND

The wind is
air in motion.
It blows from
four directions:
north, south,
east, and west.
March winds can
be chilly or mild,
as they blow the
cold winter air
away. It's a
great month to
fly a kite!

I rise out of bed
And move overhead.
Gently I spread
A blanket of gold.

As I float higher,
I fill the entire
Sky with my fire,
So you won't get cold.

What am I?

THE SUN

The summer sun is hottest of all, because it is straight overhead. In other seasons, the earth is tilted and the sun's rays are slanted.

You can't help but hear me.
Mumbleclapcrash!

It's easy to fear me.
Grumbleslapflash!

If you ever got near me
Rumblesnapsmash!

You would easily see
That under my thunder
Is electricity.

What am I?

A THUNDERSTORM

Both thunder
and lightning
are caused by
electricity in
clouds. Lightning
sometimes
strikes tall trees
or buildings that
are wet from
the storm. That
is because
electricity travels
better through
water than air.

Finally I'm free
From my trap in a tree!
My escape
Changed my shape
And my movement.

I don't crawl anymore.
My new wings let me soar
Like a kite!
It is quite
An improvement.

What am I?

A BUTTERFLY

The "trap" in which a caterpillar stays before becoming a butterfly is called a *chrysalis,* or cocoon. Animals that change forms are said to go through *metamorphosis.*

Blink,
We're off.

Blink,
We're on.

Wink,
We're here.

Wink,
We're gone.

Lights in flight.
Stars in a jar.
Do you know who we are?

FIREFLIES

When fireflies flash in the night, they are communicating with one another. The glow comes from a coating on their tails.

I'm green,
Then I'm red,
Or goldish,
Or brown.

Sometimes I'm up.
Sometimes I'm down.

I can be round,
Or pointed,
Or wispy.

I'm soft when I'm new,
But when I'm old?
Crispy!

What am I?

A LEAF

Leaves change color in the fall for two reasons: there is less daylight and more cold air than in either the spring or the summer.

Small, gray, and furry,
I hurry and scurry
During the fall,
Gathering all
The nuts I can hold
To eat when it's cold.

What am I?

A SQUIRREL

Squirrels also like to eat seeds, but sometimes forget where they've buried them. In time, the seeds take root and grow into plants.

Munch me at snack time,
Crunch me at lunch.
I'm sweet and I'm juicy,
And I have a hunch
You'll rate my varieties
Equally high,
When cooked in a sauce
Or baked in a pie.

What am I?

AN APPLE

Apples are good
to eat. They
have lots of
vitamins. Their
crunchy texture
also helps to
keep your teeth
and mouth
clean.

We look like a V,
Or maybe a Y,
As away we all go,
Away we all fly.
Far from the snow
And each wintry storm—
To stay where it's warm.

What are we?

MIGRATING BIRDS

How do birds that travel south stay on the right path? Scientists say they use clues, such as the sun and the stars, to guide them.

I fall to the ground,
But I never break.

I sit very softly
On a frozen lake.

I stick to your mitten
But I'm off with a shake.

I'm one-of-a-kind
Because I'm a _____.

SNOWFLAKE

No two snowflakes are alike, but every one has six sides. The warmer the air, the bigger the snowflake.

Unlike the others—
Our birch and beech brothers,
Red oaks and the rest—
All year long, we stay dressed!

What are we?

EVERGREEN TREES

Evergreens shed needles—a few at a time—throughout the year. New needles grow in to replace the lost ones.

What glitters like diamonds,
But has no price?

What's sharp as a dagger,
But not used to slice?

What hangs from the shingles
In rows neat and nice?

(Now, be precise.
It's not just ice.)

ICICLES

Icicles are made
from melting
snow that drips
off trees, tall
rocks, or
rooftops, and
then freezes
again.

What's another name for resting
All through the winter season?
Bears do it just by instinct
And for no other reason.

They eat for weeks beforehand.
They need energy to save
For the months they will be sleeping
Inside a cozy cave.

On mornings when it's freezing
And you'd rather stay in bed,
Don't you wish you weren't a person,
And could be a bear instead?

What do bears do in winter?

THEY HIBERNATE

Porcupines, snakes, bats, and frogs all hibernate, too. They wake up refreshed and ready for fun, when spring comes again.